TOTALLY
SUNFLOWERS

To Omy, who gives me roses.

Celestial Arts Publishing
P.O. Box 7123
Berkeley, CA 94707

Cover design and illustration: Bob Greisen
Interior design and typesetting: Susan Hernday
Interior illustrations: Carolyn Vibbert

Totally Sunflowers is produced by becker&mayer!, Ltd.

Printed in Singapore

ISBN 0-89087-783-1
Library of Congress Catalog Card Number: 95-71817

First Printing, 1996

1 2 3 4 / 99 98 97 96

Other books in the Totally Flowers series:
Totally Tulips
Totally Orchids
Totally Roses

TOTALLY SUNFLOWERS

By Joanna Poncavage

Illustrated by
Carolyn Vibbert

CELESTIAL ARTS
BERKELEY, CALIFORNIA

CONTENTS

INTRODUCTION

Kansas is nicknamed "The Sunflower State," and a wild sunflower is the state's official flower. In the law proclaiming this fact, passed in 1903, the state legislature extolled this weed to be "a flower that a child can draw on a slate, a woman can work in silk, or a man can carve in stone or fashion in clay... This flower has to all Kansans a historic symbolism which speaks of frontier days, winding trails, pathless prairies, and is full of life and glory of the past, the pride of the present, and richly emblematic of the majesty of a golden future..."

WHY SUNFLOWERS?

Sunflowers are the "happy faces" of the 1990s. Could it have all begun in 1987 when van Gogh's "Sunflowers" sold for a record-breaking $40 million?

SUNFLOWERS ARE SUN-WORSHIPPERS

Their countenances follow the sun across the sky from morning to evening, an ability botanists call "heliotropism." Perhaps our enchantment with sunflowers is really a nostalgic longing for the days when we, too, could bask in the sun without a coating of SPF45 sunscreen.

Sunflowers are Garden Stars

Whatever their place in popular culture, it is in the New American Garden that sunflowers find their true calling. In this decade of low-maintenance, natural landscapes, sunflowers have come home. They are easy to grow and they have many uses as mixed plantings, informal garden borders, backdrops, or privacy hedges. They are among the most striking of cut flowers. You can grow them for food, too—their seeds are tasty and nutritious. In fact, there's not a bird alive that can resist a feeder stocked with sunflower seeds.

SUNFLOWERS ARE PATRIOTIC

Sunflowers are front-runners in the native plant/wildflower craze. At least one kind of sunflower—and there are many—grows wild in each of the United States. Domesticated by Native Americans, probably in the fertile Midwest, sunflowers have been grown on this continent for food, oil, and fiber—and maybe just for their beauty—for 4,000 years. They are a flower with a history, a heritage, and an all-American rating. In fact, it would be more accurate to say "as American as a sunflower" rather than "as American as apple pie"— because apples are originally natives to Central Asia.

SUNFLOWERS EXPLAINED

All of the world's fifty species of sunflowers belong to the genus *Helianthus*, a name derived from the Greek *helios*, meaning sun, and *anthos*, meaning flower. Most are native to North America, and their range extends from deserts to prairies, woodlands to swamps, and from sea level to mountainsides. Most are annuals, but some are perennials. Plant sizes and shapes vary as well, from tall, single-stem lollipops to short, chubby bushes. Some sunflower blooms are the size of soup-spoons; some are the size of dinner platters.

Sunflowers are members of the "composite," or daisy family. Sunflower cousins include strawflowers, cosmos, asters, and lettuce. Flowers of plants in this family have round, flat centers surrounded by a radiating halo of petals. Pollen and seeds are produced in the centers. The petals around the centers are brightly colored to help bees find the pollen needed to cross-pollinate with flowers on the other side of the garden. Many beneficial insects and butterflies visit sunflowers for their pollen as well. Yellow is the predominant sunflower color.

THE PRETTIEST SUNFLOWERS

Many modern sunflowers were bred for beauty. Most are the branching, multiple-headed (polycephalic) type, with many four- to eight-inch flowers covering their bushy shapes. In recent years, these decorative sunflowers have proliferated in shades of mahogany, bronze, red, sunset orange, lemon yellow, pale yellow, creamy white, and nearly pure white. Breeding is centered in Europe and Japan, and new, more fanciful varieties are appearing in seed catalogs each year.

AUTUMN BEAUTY is the sunflower to grow if you only have space for one. It will feed the birds, it will look pretty in your garden, and it will astound as a cut flower. One packet of seeds will give you an exquisite range of fall colors, from copper red to reddish purple. Stalks can grow up to six feet tall (heights and growth habits vary), and are ideal for a beautiful privacy hedge.

COLOR FASHION MIX is a bright blend of yellows, reds, and purples. Plants grow to six feet tall and tend to be single-stemmed with only a few side branches. Flowers can be five or more inches across.

Park's VELVET TAPESTRY produces uniform, six-inch flowers with brown centers and rich, deep, velvety crimson petals highlighted with gold. Color combinations vary—some flowers are all red, some are red touched with gold, and some are mostly gold with a red blush. Plants grow five to six feet tall, and are very bushy and branched.

SOUTHERN LIGHTS is a multicolored mixture with a wide range of colors. Some flowers are pure lemon yellow, some are gold, and some are bicolored combinations of gold, burgundy, and brown. Centers vary from dark brown to black. Flowers are about five inches across, and plants will grow four feet tall. Their stalks have many branches.

Music Box is a delightful sunflower that grows only twenty-eight inches tall, but its short plants are covered with four-inch flowers in creamy white to yellow, red, and mahogany. Each flower sports a black center. You should plant this one if you want dramatic accents in small spaces, or vibrant color in arrangements.

Floristan adds a new dimension to sunflower colors—its short petals are reddish brown tipped with yellow and its big, wide-eyed centers are dark brown. Plants are three to four feet tall and flowers are four to six inches across.

INCA JEWELS is an early-blooming (sixty days) mixture of five or more flower types in magnificent jewel colors. Flowers are various shades of yellow, some with halos ranging from maroon to red-brown and copper. These flowers are five to six inches across with large, burnt orange centers. Plants have one primary stem, with secondary branches emerging from its upper third. Stalk color varies from pure green to green with heavy purple streaks. INCA JEWELS makes a wonderful cut flower or border.

CLASSIC COLORS

If you want classic sunflowers—yellow petals around a brown disk—try these:

HOLIDAY has three- to five-inch blooms born profusely on multibranching plants that can grow five to seven feet tall.

TAIYO has bright yellow petals around wide, dark centers. Stalks are six feet tall.

HENRY WILDE is an exceptionally tall ornamental sunflower, with stalks eight to ten feet tall. Flowers have butter yellow petals around a deep chocolate disk. The main stems bear one large flower and up to fifteen smaller blooms.

PALE FACES

MOONWALKER is a vigorous, four- to five-foot grower. The branching plants each have six to ten flowers of various diameters, with pale lemon yellow petals around chocolate brown centers.

VALENTINE has six- to eight-inch flowers with soft lemon yellow petals surrounding a central black disk. Plants grow about five feet tall, and branch at the base to produce strong, uniform thirty-inch stems for each flower. VALENTINE blooms early and keeps on blooming over a long period of time.

LEMON QUEEN is a bushy five- to seven-foot plant that sends up many branches, each bearing lots of five-inch citron yellow flowers with dark chocolate centers. With this flower, a single stem is often a whole arrangement.

WHITE SUNFLOWERS

Be cool! Grow white sunflowers! These elegant flowers are formal enough for a black-tie affair. There's VANILLA ICE, with pale cream petals surrounding a rich, dark brown center. Plants grow to a bushy six feet; the flowers are a neat six inches across.

ITALIAN WHITE has soft, slightly feathery, creamy white petals around a dark chocolate center; flowers are about five inches across and plants only grow to five feet tall. ITALIAN WHITES flower over a long period of time, and their blooms have long, straight stems for elegant arrangements.

RED AND VIBRANT

Then there are the reds! VELVET QUEEN has velvety, dark burgundy petals around a charcoal-black center. Multiple branches support strong stems and many, many vibrant flowers. This variety grows up to six feet tall, and is outstanding when grown in a hedge for a border or for cutting.

PRADO RED produces fifteen to twenty deep mahogany flowers with dark yellow centers per plant, many on the same branched stem. Plants grow five to six feet tall, and flowers are five to six inches across. Available from Territorial Seed Co., these are the reddest sunflowers you can grow.

Many of the red sunflower varieties can trace their ancestry back to a mutant red sunflower found growing along a Colorado road in 1910.

SHAGGY SUNFLOWERS

Some sunflowers look like fluffy floor mops. These are called "double" sunflowers because of the overabundant petals. These are spectacular when used for cut flowers.

TEDDY BEAR's shaggy double blooms are bright yellow, and are about five inches across. The plants themselves are compact, and reach about three to four feet in height.

GIANT SUNGOLD blooms are eight inches across—yes, they really are giants! These heavy golden heads are borne on six-foot stalks.

Perfect for large arrangements, ORANGE SUN bears six- to eight-inch fluffy, orange, double flowers on four-foot plants.

LION'S MANE produces a half-dozen soft, intense, orange petal-covered six-inch flowers per six-foot stalk.

WORKS IN PROGRESS

DISCOVERY MIX is an exciting surprise package of works in progress from Seeds of Change, a New Mexico seed company. Seeds in DISCOVERY MIX are the result of a cross between GLORIOSA, a multiheaded sunflower with blooms that look like Gloriosa daisies with brilliant red bull's-eyes, and LION'S MANE, a tall, mostly single-stemmed sunflower with orange, shaggy, double flowers. Their

offspring are some of the finest and most
unusual sunflowers available—doubles with
red color in them, singles with red, orange,
tawny, and lemon markings.

THE FUZZY SUNFLOWER

The silver leaves of the DIASETSUZAN sunflower
are very soft with a white, fuzzy coating. This
unusual sunflower will grow into a large,
nine-foot, well-branched plant. Its flowers are
a uniform four to five inches across, and are
gold with black centers. Even though the
plant has a branching habit, its blooms can
be used for cut flowers because their stems
are long. Flowers are produced over a thirty-
day period, which is unusual for annual
sunflowers.

POLLENLESS SUNFLOWERS

Pollen is beloved by bees and other insects, but in an effort to keep it from coating your dining room table with a fine layer of fertile dust, plant breeders have been busy developing purely decorative, pollenless hybrids. These flowers are good for your cleaning bills, but frustrating for birds because the seeds of these plants are just empty shells.

SUNBEAM, one of the new pollenless types, has an unusual chartreuse center surrounded by golden yellow petals. Plants reach five feet tall and the early-blooming flowers are five inches across. Mix with fine-leafed, frilly foliage for eye-opening arrangements.

Sunrich Orange and Sunrich Lemon are two new sunflower classics. Sunrich Orange has golden yellow petals, and Sunrich Lemon has petals of a clear yellow tone. Both have coal black centers unmuddied by dusty pollen. Both bear blooms that are five to six inches across on single stems about four feet tall.

Full Sun is a six-foot version of the classic van Gogh type of sunflower found in Dutch flower stalls. Flowers have golden yellow petals surrounding a brown, pollenless center.

Sunbright has the classic sunflower color scheme—bright, golden yellow petals around a dark brown, pollenless center. Stalks grow five to six feet tall.

SHORT STUFF

One of the oddest sunflowers, SUNSPOT is a dwarf plant with a huge flower. Stocky stalks barely stretch two feet tall, but the flowers can be almost one foot across. Children love SUNSPOT—it's just their size. It's a natural choice for small gardens and containers, too.

SONJA is another diminutive sunflower. Plants reach only about three feet tall. With a neat, branching habit, these sunflowers produce four-inch, tangerine-colored blooms with brown centers that are sturdy, long-lasting, and perfect for cutting. They will shine wherever you plant them, in borders or containers.

HOW TO GROW STELLAR SUNFLOWERS

Sunflowers are extremely easy to grow. Their seeds are nice and big, and easy to poke into the ground. Germination is quick and dependable. They require full sun, but they will grow in rich or poor soil, and once they're established, they will tolerate arid conditions. Sunflowers just aren't very fussy.

But be warned: If you share your garden with critters (and who doesn't?), protect tasty sunflower seedlings with a floating row cover until they can take care of themselves.

WHERE TO PLANT

There's no need to plant sunflowers in little peat pots or containers indoors before setting them out into a waiting garden. Unlike many plants that need a head start indoors, sunflowers don't cotton to being moved around a lot, or transplanted once they are past a certain age. They grow so quickly, you might miss this window of opportunity. Also, sowing sunflowers directly into the garden helps them develop a stronger root system for better support. This is especially important for the taller varieties.

For best results, seed your sunflowers where you want them to bloom.

When to Plant

Sunflowers prefer to grow in warm weather. You can begin to sow their seeds outdoors up to two weeks before the last frost date for your area. Nighttime temperatures above 55 degrees F is ideal. A good rule of thumb is to plant sunflowers when it's time to plant corn. They like the same conditions—lots of warmth, lots of moisture with good drainage, and lots of room.

Depth and Spacing

Plant seeds about an inch deep. If you plant them in rows, space the rows one to three feet apart, depending on the expected size of the variety. Thin them to stand one foot apart when they are four to six inches tall.

GETTING THE MOST FLOWERS

Branching sunflowers will cover themselves with the most blooms if you plant them in soil that is not too rich. This means you don't need to add any extra compost or aged manure to your garden before planting sunflower seeds. In fact, the secret for getting many flowers from any plant is to keep it hungry. A soil that is too rich fosters the growth of leaves, not flowers. Here's another trick: Sunflowers will produce more flowers and fewer leaves (it's the biological imperative to reproduce under hardship) if you don't overwater them. Give them less-than-lush conditions and they'll give you a better show.

Branching sunflowers provide a long season of bloom, especially if you cut flowers now and then for indoor arrangements. Remove the spent flowers ("dead-heading"), too. If you plan on doing a lot of cutting, and want lots of sunflowers, consider growing your plants in a "cutting garden." This just means that you can lop and chop away at the stems, and not worry about the appearance of what you leave behind. Hide your cutting garden behind the garage, or behind a hedge of tall, monster sunflowers. Sow a new row of cutting sunflowers every couple weeks for nonstop arrangements. This way, a new patch of sunflowers will always be ready for cutting just as an old section is starting to fade.

PLANTING VARIATIONS

If you grow sunflowers in a tight space, the plants will stay small. This works especially well with single-headed sunflowers. Space them closely, and you will get miniature versions of any variety. Take FULL SUN, for example. This is a classic sunflower, with a dark brown to black center surrounded by golden, pointed petals. Given unlimited space, it will grow up to ten feet tall, and its flowers will span fourteen inches across. Space them four or five inches apart, however, and you'll get a pretty cut-flower candidate that's four to six inches across, on a stem that's only a few feet long. Just right for a big bouquet of flowers in an oversize vase.

HOW TO CUT SUNFLOWERS

Sunflowers will last up to two weeks in a vase if you follow these instructions:

- The best time to cut sunflowers is morning or late evening, but you can cut them any time of the day; if they wilt, they'll revive.
- Cut the stems with garden scissors or a knife. Flowers not fully open when you cut them will open up in the vase.
- Take a bucket of lukewarm water (about 100–105 degrees F) with you into the garden, and plunge the stems into the water immediately after cutting.
- When arranging the sunflowers, remove all

but the top two or three leaves from the stems. This provides less opportunity for bacteria to grow in the vase.

- To keep sunflowers fresh, change their water frequently (at least every other day) and add a couple of drops of bleach each time. This also helps prevent the growth of bacteria that might clog the stems.
- Cut sunflowers will last the longest if they are kept cool and in the shade. If you need to save them for a special occasion, a refrigerator is ideal.

SUNFLOWER BOUQUETS

Sunflowers have such presence, anything you mix with them in a bouquet is in danger of being upstaged. To give sunflowers the lead, arrange them with delicate fillers such as flowering herbs like mint, purple basil, or native grasses. Sunflowers with Queen Anne's lace is a pretty combination, too.

Blue or purple flowers are especially attractive in combination with yellow sunflowers. Try combinations with larkspur, butterfly bush, or purple coneflower.

Big stalks of sunflowers do very well in tall, thin vases or jars. Set them in front of a fireplace, or in any corner or hallway in need of a little brightness.

EDIBLE SUNFLOWERS

Sunflowers are agricultural workhorses. Millions of acres of sunflowers are grown worldwide each year for their seeds. Most of these seeds are crushed to produce a valuable edible oil. The rest are used for snacks, baked goods, cereals, and bird food. Not to mention that they provide baseball players a healthy alternative to chewing tobacco.

Sunflowers grown for their seeds have big yellow flowers. Some monsters have eighteen-inch seed heads atop twelve-foot, sapling-like stems. If you plant these big sunflowers, sow them on the north side of your garden so they don't shade the sun from your tomatoes, or simply grow them along the sunny side of a building.

THE GIANTS

The tallest of these sunflowers will have words like "giant" or "mammoth" in their names. GIANT GREY STRIPE (also called MAMMOTH GREY STRIPE) can grow twelve to fifteen feet tall under optimum conditions. Heads can be fifteen inches across. Seeds are broad, with white and gray stripes.

MAMMOTH RUSSIAN is an old favorite that actually did originate in Russia, and was first sold in America in the 1880s. Stalks can reach twelve or more feet tall, and flower heads can be up to twelve inches across. Seeds are large and meaty, with thin, striped shells.

One of the biggest sunflowers is also one of the newest. Aptly called PAUL BUNYAN, this garden behemoth can tower up to fifteen feet tall. Flower heads can be twenty inches across, filled with large black or white seeds. Available only from W. Atlee Burpee Co., this giant was developed over an eleven-year period of breeding and selection from parents adapted to tropical Africa.

Another good variety to grow for edible seeds is JUMBO. Heads can be fourteen or more inches across on eight-foot-tall plants. The large black seeds have white stripes, are broad and uniform, and measure half an inch wide and five-eighths of an inch long.

PEREDOVIK is a black-seeded, commercial Russian variety grown for oil and birdseed mixes. This is also one of the best varieties to grow if you want seeds for snacking and cooking, because the seed shells are so thin they can sometimes be cracked by hand, and are easily removed by machine (see page 49). Stalks often reach six feet tall, with occasional side branches. Seed heads vary from four to six inches across. (To find out why so many sunflowers have a Russian past, see page 88.)

SUNFLOWERS FROM THE SOUTHWEST

Native tribes of the American Southwest and Mexico have long depended on sunflowers for food, fiber, and dye. HAVASUPAI STRIPED comes from the gardens of the Havasupai Indians at the bottom of the Grand Canyon. Stalks are seven feet tall with seed heads about eight inches across, with some smaller blooms. Their long, narrow black-and-white striped seeds are good for snacking or bird food. Among thousands of sunflowers tested by the USDA, HAVASUPAI STRIPED showed nearly complete resistance to a troublesome rust disease. Its genes have been transferred to other sunflowers, eliminating the need for chemical fungicides.

TARAHUMARA WHITE is an unusual, especially attractive sunflower with all-white seeds. Brought to Mexico by Mennonites from Canada, it has been cultivated by the Tarahumara tribe of Chihuahua for decades, and it's become adapted to both low and high desert conditions. Large flowers are a solid, glowing gold, twelve or more inches across with stalks up to seven feet tall. Seeds are large and easily cracked. Most plants bear one single, large flower, but there can be smaller side blooms.

A mature sunflower head has from 250 to 1,500 seeds arranged in a spiral pattern.

APACHE BROWN STRIPED has eight-inch heads, eight-foot stalks, and medium-sized seeds that are white with brown stripes. It is traditionally grown in the low desert conditions of the San Carlos Reservation in Arizona, making it a variety tough enough to grow almost anywhere.

HOPI BLACK DYE has purple-black seeds used by the Hopis to make dye, but this variety is excellent for eating, too. It doesn't tolerate a lot of rain and humidity, but it produces lots of seeds with shells that are thin and easily removed. Plants grow six feet tall with nine-inch seed heads. Flowers are composed of yellow petals surrounding attractive purple-green centers. Stems also have a purplish color.

SUNFLOWERS TO DYE FOR

HOPI BLACK DYE sunflower is the source of deep blue, purple, black, or red dyes used to color baskets, pottery, and woolens. According to Mary Russell Ferrell Colton in her book *Hopi Dyes*, the process begins by burning yellow ochre (a natural ore) with piñon tree gum. This makes the iron in the yellow ochre water-soluble. The resulting charcoal-like substance is ground into a powder. Black sunflower seeds are then boiled in order to extract their tannin. When the sunflower liquid is mixed with the black powder (along with natural alum), the result is an inky permanent dye.

HOW TO GROW BIG SUNFLOWERS

Big sunflowers need a frost-free growing season of at least 120 days to mature and produce nice, fat, tasty seeds. Sow them about two weeks before the last spring frost in your area, and they will bloom in late July or August. They'll be ready for a fall harvest in September or October.

- Select a variety with giant in its genes—something like PAUL BUNYAN, MAMMOTH RUSSIAN, RUSSIAN GIANT, or MAMMOTH GREY STRIPE.
- Before planting, prepare your garden bed by digging a couple of inches of compost or thoroughly aged manure into the soil.

- Sow the seeds directly into the soil one inch deep about two weeks before the last frost is expected in your area. Sow seeds in clusters of three or four; clip off all but the most vigorous one from each cluster.
- Give your plants plenty of room to grow by providing at least three feet of space in all directions.
- Give your plants plenty of water and fertilize once a week with fish emulsion.
- Tie stalks to sturdy stakes as they grow, in order to protect them from strong winds. Another way to keep them upright is to mound up soil around their base.

HOW TO HARVEST A SUNFLOWER

Birds will be birds, so to save the sunflower seeds you want for yourself, cover the sunflower heads with netting, cheesecloth, old pillow cases, or brown paper bags as the seeds begin to develop. Sunflower seeds are ripe when the little pollen-bearing florets that cover the center fall off, exposing the dry, plump seeds beneath them. Other signs that the seeds are ripe: The yellow petals surrounding the seed center fade, dry, and fall off; the back of the sunflower head turns from green to yellow to brown; and birds are starting to eat the seeds.

When all the seeds in the center of the sunflower are plump and full (seeds mature from the outside in), cut the heads from the stalks. To remove the seeds from the flower heads, hold the head face toward you with two hands and bend the sides back. Work the seeds loose with your thumbs and collect them in a bowl or basket. A stiff wire brush can help remove seeds, too. Spread the seeds in a thin layer and dry thoroughly in a warm, airy, shady spot for several weeks. Indoors is best, because all kinds of creatures will help themselves otherwise.

GROW YOUR OWN BEAN POLES

The tall, single-stemmed sunflowers can be useful, living supports for other plants to grow on. Give sunflowers a head start of at least a month, then plant three or four pole-bean seeds close to the base of the sunflower. They'll grow up together so you can pick beans without bending over!

Save the stalks of this year's MAMMOTH RUSSIAN or PAUL BUNYAN sunflowers and recycle them as support stakes for next year's bean patch. After frost kills the plant, cut and trim the stalks. Store them under cover during the winter. Next spring, tie four or five together at one end and prop them upright, teepee fashion. Sow pole beans at the bottom of each leg.

Now what?

Unless you plan to crack and eat the seeds one by one (which is not a bad thing to do, provided you have the time and patience), you'll need some mechanical intervention to get those tasty kernels out of their shells. Southern Exposure Seed Exchange (see "Resources" on page 93) sells an attachment for the Corona grain mill that hulls sunflower seeds very nicely. HOPI DYE, PEREDOVIK, or some other conical-shaped, black-seeded sunflower variety will work best. Store sunflower seeds, in or out of the hull, in airtight containers, and they'll stay fresh for up to four months.

SUNFLOWERS IN THE KITCHEN

A NUTRITIONAL POWERHOUSE

Sunflower seeds are some of the most healthful foods you can eat. They contain high-quality protein with all the essential amino acids. They are a good source of several important nutrients such as vitamin E, vitamin B6, folate, zinc, magnesium, potassium, and thiamin. Sunflower seeds have twice the iron of raisins and peanuts. Every one-ounce serving of sunflower seeds provides four grams of dietary fiber—the fiber equivalent to a serving of bran flakes. An added bonus is that they taste good, with a flavor that's a delicate combination of toasted pecan and buttered popcorn.

OIL'S WELL

Like other fats from vegetable sources, the oil in sunflower seeds is seventy percent poly-unsaturated (more than soy, corn, or olive oils) and contains no cholesterol. What's more, sunflower oil is high in linoleic acid, an essential fatty acid linked to lower blood cholesterol levels, and it contains more vitamin E than any other common oil.

Sunflower oil has a delicate, light color and taste. In fact, sunflower is the oil of choice for most of the world, including Europe, South America, and North Africa. It can be heated to a higher temperature (450 degrees F) than other oils before it begins to smoke. This means it won't add unpleasant flavors to high-temperature cooking, such as a stir-fry. It's also perfect for salad dressings, baked goods, and it makes a nice margarine.

ROASTED SUNFLOWER SEEDS

Spread a single layer of raw, unshelled kernels in a shallow pan. Place pan in oven and bake at 300 degrees F for 30 to 40 minutes, depending on desired toastiness. Roasted seeds can be substituted for nuts in any recipe, or sprinkled on salads. Sunflower seeds are especially complementary to green peppers.

For zesty snacking, season 2 cups of hot, roasted seeds with $\frac{1}{2}$ teaspoon of melted margarine, $\frac{1}{2}$ teaspoon of Worcestershire sauce, $\frac{1}{8}$ teaspoon chile powder, and $\frac{1}{8}$ teaspoon garlic powder. Mix well and spread out across paper towels to dry. Store tightly covered, for roasted seeds do not store as long as raw seeds.

SUNFLOWER PESTO

8 ounces tomato, spinach, or plain spaghetti
3 parsley sprigs
3 garlic cloves
$1/2$ cup fresh basil leaves
$1/4$ cup sunflower oil
$2/3$ cup grated Parmesan cheese
$1/2$ cup roasted sunflower kernels
$1/4$ teaspoon salt
freshly ground pepper

Cook spaghetti according to package directions and drain. Mince parsley, basil, and garlic. Toss into hot pasta, adding sunflower oil, sunflower kernels, cheese, salt, and pepper.

SERVES 4

"BLACK HILLS" TUNA SANDWICHES

2 tablespoons mayonnaise
1 tablespoon yogurt
1/2 teaspoon dried mixed herbs
    or 1 tablespoon fresh
salt and freshly ground pepper
4 lettuce leaves, washed and dried
4 large slices tomato
1/3 cup roasted sunflower seeds, coarsely
    chopped
1 green onion, finely chopped
1 can tuna, drained
1 1/2 teaspoons lemon juice
4 slices pumpernickel *or* whole grain bread
4 slices sunflower *or* white bread

Mix mayonnaise, yogurt, herbs, and salt and pepper to taste. Mix tuna, lemon juice, green onion, and sunflower kernels. Spread pumpernickel or whole grain bread with yogurt-mayonnaise mixture. Top with lettuce leaves and cover with tuna spread. Top with tomato slices and additional sunflower seeds, and cover with sunflower or white bread. Cut into quarters and arrange, cut-side out.

SERVES 4

SUNFLOWER WHEAT BREAD

$1\frac{1}{2}$ cups whole wheat flour
1 cup all-purpose flour
$\frac{1}{2}$ cup quick-cooking rolled oats
$\frac{1}{2}$ cup brown sugar, packed
1 tablespoon finely shredded orange peel
$\frac{1}{2}$ teaspoon baking powder
$\frac{1}{2}$ teaspoon salt
$1\frac{3}{4}$ cups buttermilk
1 egg, slightly beaten
$\frac{1}{2}$ cup sunflower kernels
honey and sunflower kernels for garnish

Combine the first seven ingredients in a large bowl and mix well. Add milk and egg and stir until ingredients are just moistened. Stir in the sunflower kernels. Pour mixture into a greased 9 x 5-inch bread pan and bake at 350 degrees F for 50 minutes, or until a knife inserted into the center of the loaf comes out clean. Cover with foil, if necessary, to prevent over-browning. Cool in the pan for 10 minutes, then turn out onto a wire rack to cool thoroughly before cutting. Brush the top with honey and sprinkle on sunflower kernels, if desired.

MAKES 1 LOAF

EUROPEAN CHOCOLATE SUNFLOWER CAKE

$^2/_3$ cup raw sunflower kernels
$^3/_4$ cup all-purpose flour
3 tablespoons cocoa
2 teaspoons baking powder
3 eggs plus 2 egg whites
$^3/_4$ cup granulated sugar
$^1/_4$ teaspoon salt
$^1/_4$ cup sunflower oil
$^1/_4$ cup red currant or raspberry jelly
vanilla filling (recipe follows)
chocolate icing (recipe follows)
roasted sunflower kernels for garnish

Cover the bottoms of two round 9-inch cake pans with waxed paper. Grease the sides of the pans and the waxed paper.

Process the sunflower kernels to a coarse flour consistency in a blender or food processor. Sift together the flour, cocoa, and baking powder and mix with the ground sunflower kernels. Set aside.

Separate the eggs. Beat 5 egg whites and salt until stiff. Beat oil with the egg yolks, then add to the whites with the sugar. Continue beating until mixed. Fold into the flour mixture. Pour into pans. Bake at 350 degrees F for 15 minutes, turn out onto racks, peel off the waxed paper. Cool.

Take one cooled cake section and place it top-down on a plate. Spread jelly over the cake, then spread with vanilla filling. Top with second cake layer. Frost top and sides of cake with chocolate icing. Sprinkle the top of the cake with roasted sunflower kernels.

VANILLA FILLING: In top of double boiler, mix $1/3$ cup sugar, 3 tablespoons flour, and $1/4$ teaspoon salt. Gradually blend in 1 slightly beaten egg, 2 slightly beaten egg yolks, and 1 cup warmed milk, stirring until smooth. Cook and stir until the mixture thickens. Remove from heat and stir in 1 teaspoon vanilla. Cool to room temperature.

CHOCOLATE ICING: In top of double boiler, melt 1 tablespoon butter and 4 ounces semisweet chocolate. Add ⅓ cup whipping cream and mix well using a wire whisk. Remove from heat and add 1¾ cups powdered sugar and 1 teaspoon vanilla.

SERVES 8 TO 12

Germany imports more than 16,000 tons of sunflower seeds annually, many of which are used to make sunflower kernel bread, a German favorite. Spain, the second-largest importer of U.S. sunflower seeds, prefers them as roasted, salted-in-the-shell snacks.

SUNFLOWER SPROUTS

Sprouts are a nutritional powerhouse. All the energy, vitamins, and minerals a seed carries to begin a new plant are unleashed when the seed germinates. In fact, sprouts contain more protein than the seeds from which they grow. Sunflower sprouts are an incredibly tasty way to eat your homegrown sunflower seeds without shelling them. The little plant actually shells itself for you, from the inside out.

To sprout sunflower seeds, you'll need:
- a clear glass jar with a wide mouth
- a piece of cheesecloth or nylon-mesh fabric
- a rubber band
- sunflower seeds (in the shell, see page 46).

Soak the seeds in water for six to eight hours.

Discard any that float, and drain and rinse the good ones. Sterilize the jar in boiling water. Cover the bottom of the jar with a single layer of seeds. Attach the cheesecloth or mesh to the mouth of the jar with the rubber band. On a dish or tray, prop the jar at an oblique angle to drain as much water as possible from the seeds. Place the jar out of direct sunlight in a spot neither too warm nor too cold (a moderate room temperature).

Rinse the seeds with tepid water (about 70 degrees F) and drain as thoroughly as you can at least twice a day, more frequently if possible. Discard any moldy seeds. You'll get crunchy sprouts in eight to ten days. They will turn green if you place the jar in brighter light for a day. Wash the split shells away from the sprouts and discard. Add sunflower sprouts to salads, breads, soups, or a stir-fry.

SPECIAL NOTE: Sprout only seeds you've grown yourself or seeds that have not been coated with fungicides or other chemicals to assist germination. Seeds sold in bulk for bird food are fine.

JERUSALEM ARTICHOKES
THE SUNFLOWER
UNDERGROUND

The Jerusalem artichoke, or *Helianthus tuberosus*, is neither from Jerusalem nor is it an artichoke. The "Jerusalem" designation is a corruption of the Italian (and Spanish) word for sunflower, *girasol*, and the "artichoke" part comes from a similarity in taste to the classic artichoke (it tastes a little like water chestnuts, too). The edible part of the Jerusalem artichoke is a tuber that grows belowground. Sometimes called "sunchokes," these tubers are a great source of carbohydrate for diabetics.

Jerusalem artichokes are grown from tubers sold in almost any garden seed catalog. Plant them four inches deep and one foot apart in rows that are at least three feet apart. The tubers will grow, develop, and multiply throughout the summer. Come fall (a good frost improves their flavor), dig the tubers from the base of the plant. They don't store very well in the refrigerator (a maximum of one week or so in the vegetable drawer), so dig them as needed. If you mulch the row heavily with straw to keep the ground from freezing, you can dig them up throughout the winter. Eat a lot of them, because new plants will sprout from any tubers still in the ground come spring.

Jerusalem artichokes are also ornamental. Their plants grow big and bushy, and can reach up to twelve feet tall. Hundreds of dainty and attractive flowers—with clear lemon yellow petals surrounding a yellow center—will cover each plant. They bloom in late summer, at a time when any kind of flower is a welcome sight in some parts of the country.

Jerusalem artichokes are perennial plants, so if you have the space, give them a permanent bed all their own. Just be sure it's somewhere they won't become a problem if they spread out a little.

ROAST CHICKEN WITH JERUSALEM ARTICHOKES AND LEEKS

1 small roasting chicken (a whole fryer will do)
2 cups Jerusalem artichokes
4 leeks
2 tablespoons chopped fresh, *or* 2 teaspoons crumbled dried herbs (a mix of tarragon, sage, or rosemary works well)
salt and pepper

Wash the chicken inside and out and place in a small roasting pan. Scrub the Jerusalem artichokes. Cut the tops off the leeks, slice lengthwise and wash away any grit hiding in the crevices. Place the herbs inside the chicken; season with salt and pepper; add artichokes and leeks to the pan. Roast at 350 degrees F until done, about 20 minutes per pound; juices will run clear. Arrange the carved chicken on a platter along with the roasted vegetables. Add $\frac{1}{3}$ cup white wine to the defatted roasting pan juices, simmer briefly, and drizzle over all.

JERUSALEM ARTICHOKE LATKES

2 cups grated Jerusalem artichokes
1/4 cup grated onion
1 egg, slightly beaten
1/2 cup matzo meal
salt and pepper

Mix all ingredients. Heat griddle to medium high and spray with nonstick vegetable oil. Drop by spoonfuls and brown on both sides. Serve with sour cream and applesauce.

JERUSALEM ARTICHOKE PICKLES

Substitute Jerusalem artichokes in any pickle recipe. Good flavor combinations are caraway, mustard, and garlic.

UNUSUAL SUNFLOWERS

Most domesticated sunflowers are summer-blooming annuals, but some rare, exotic, perennial, wild sunflowers are edging into the ornamental garden trade.

The WILLOW-LEAF sunflower (*Helianthus salicifolius*) used to be considered a weed growing on the dry, limy soils of Missouri until a plant lover noticed its beauty. One plant sends up several six-foot stems from which droop skinny leaves that are six inches long but only one-eighth of an inch wide. The overall effect is that of a weeping willow. This sunflower will add a green fernlike fineness to the back of a garden, until great numbers of its two-inch yellow flowers bloom in late summer. It does best in soils that are not too rich.

The SHOWY SUNFLOWER *(Helianthus laeti-florus)* is a late-blooming sunflower that produces many seeds to feed plenty of birds. It will grow on medium to extremely dry soils, although it will tolerate flooding, and it spreads aggressively by subterranean rootlike plant stems called "rhizomes." It's a short-grass prairie plant, and will reach a maximum of only three feet tall.

The NAKED SUNFLOWER *(Helianthus occidentalis)* is another short-grass prairie species, often found growing with its "showy" cousin. NAKED SUNFLOWER is another short one, reaching less than three feet at maturity. Yellow flowers bloom from August to September. It does well in dry soil, including sand, and birds flock to its seeds.

The DOWNY SUNFLOWER *(Helianthus mollis)* thrives on poor, dry soils, and bears butter yellow flowers on soft, hairy stems. This robust plant reaches a bushy five feet tall and spreads by rhizomes. Birds love it!

FLORE PLENO SUNFLOWER *(Helianthus multiflorus)* is one of the more dramatic perennial sunflowers. Although its bushy plants don't grow very tall (usually less than five feet), they become covered with double yellow blooms from July through September. These are especially good for cheerful cut flowers.

SWAMP SUNFLOWER *(Helianthus angustifolius)* blooms in mid-October in the Mid-Atlantic states, bringing blazing yellow color to late fall gardens. Its abundant yellow flowers will totally cover the top third of these ten-foot plants. Cut them back by one-third in early summer to encourage more branching and more flowers. As its name infers, it will do well in a moist site, but it will grow nicely in a well-drained area, too.

WESTERN SUNFLOWER *(Helianthus occidentalis)* is another finch favorite. Its bright yellow starlike flowers top long, leafless stalks, making this wildflower a perfect candidate for rustic bouquets. Flowers appear throughout late summer; the plant spreads slowly on rhizomes in medium to extremely dry soils.

GIANT SUNFLOWER *(Helianthus giganteus)* is one of the tallest, growing up to twelve feet high. This perennial spreads by rhizomes and forms dense clumps. In late summer and early fall, its giant shape will be covered with warm, two-inch, pale yellow flowers. These flowers produce seeds that will quickly attract many goldfinches. The GIANT sunflower will grow in medium moist soil and will tolerate light shade. Like the other big sunflowers, it needs plenty of room.

Perennial Sunflowers in the Landscape

Perennial sunflowers have a longer bloom period than the domesticated annuals, and will provide a riot of yellow from midsummer through fall. Some, including the Swamp sunflower, will tolerate light frosts and continue to bloom until a hard frost.

Their flowers range through many different shades of yellow, and their brightness goes a long way in the garden, especially to make blues and other colors pop out a little better. Flowers of the different varieties tend to be about the same size, from about one to two inches across. Perennial sunflowers make good cut flowers, too. Most have several flowers per main stem. Good combinations with other native plants include joe-pye weed, boltonia, liatris, ironweed, and the grasses.

Where should you plant these perennial sunflowers? They would work fine as the tall center of an island bed, or in a meadow planting where everything runs together. Since many of them are large bushy plants, they can be combined with medium-sized true shrubs, and they would show up nicely in front of an evergreen border. They would also add late color to a combination of shrubs, because so many shrubs are spring bloomers.

You'll get the most flowers if you site perennial sunflowers where they will get at least half a day of full sun, preferably the more intense afternoon sun. For the most part, these are unfussy plants and will grow in a wide range of soils and conditions.

SUNFLOWERS FOR THE BIRDS

All sunflowers—from the perennial, wild species to the ornamentals to the food crop types—produce seeds that will bring in birds by the dozens. In fact, sunflower seeds seem to be the favorite of most seed-eating birds.

Some especially picky eaters, such as the rose-breasted grosbeak, won't accept an invitation to the bird feeder until the menu includes sunflower seeds. Chickadees, nuthatches, blue jays, and cardinals are less choosy, but will be first in line for sunflower seeds. Sunflower seeds will even attract ground-feeding birds, such as rufous-sided towhees, juncos, and sparrows, who will be happy to wait below messy eaters at the feeder.

If you are going to grow only one kind of sunflower for bird food, make it the black oil sunflower. But if you have the space, grow several kinds. Each type of sunflower produces a different size and shape of seed. The more different types of sunflowers you grow, the wider the variety of birds that will visit your yard.

The birds will help themselves to the seeds when they are fully developed if you simply let the flowers remain on the plants. Or you can harvest the dried flowers with their mature seeds, dry them some more indoors (see page 47), and dole them out to your feathered friends during the lean and hungry times. Supplemental feeding is especially important in winter when the oil in the seeds supplies much needed energy.

Here are a couple of sunflower varieties that were developed for commercial production of seeds, so they will produce lots of seeds for birds: Sundak and Arrowhead both produce stalks about six feet tall, with very few side heads. Seed heads are six or more inches across. Sundak seeds are large with black and gray stripes. Sundak is a disease-resistant variety developed at the University of Minnesota. Arrowhead is a narrow-seeded sunflower developed in the Czech Republic.

The U.S. birdfood industry uses 271,750 tons of sunflowers annually.

CRAFTY WAYS WITH SUNFLOWERS

HOW TO DRY SUNFLOWERS

You can keep sunflowers shining in vases all year long if you dry them first.

Simply cut the stems to the desired length, then hang them upside down in a dry, warm place. Loop a piece of string around each stem to attach it to a line or to hooks. Be sure to allow plenty of space between the stems for air to circulate. Attics are a good place to dry sunflowers; so are airy garages and basements. Sunflowers are dry when they become light and brittle. Arrange them in a vase by themselves, or with branches of dried autumn leaves or fresh evergreens.

You can also dry sunflower heads without the stems. Just clip them from their plants with garden shears or a knife, and lay the heads on a screen, calyx-side down (face up). When dry, use a hot glue gun to attach them to garlands or wreaths made of other plant material such as eucalyptus leaves, for example.

If conditions are damp and mildew is a problem, you can dry big sunflower heads quickly in an oven set at 150–175 degrees F. Lay the heads directly onto the oven rack, not on a cookie sheet. This method works much the same way as a food dehydrator. Keep the oven fan on to help remove the moisture.

A NATIVE AMERICAN CROP

The sunflower is the only food crop domesticated in North America still being grown today. Thousands of years ago, hunters and gatherers discovered that sunflower seeds tasted good and contained plenty of oil. These ancient people naturally harvested the heads with the biggest and best seeds, and gradually the sunflowers that sprouted around the villages, whether intentionally planted or not, had bigger and better seeds than their ancestors. This domestication probably began more than 4,000 years ago in what is now Tennessee and Kentucky.

Sunflowers were a multi-purpose crop. Native Americans ground their seeds into a meal that was mixed with cornmeal to bake thin cakes and to thicken stews. Roasted sunflower hulls were boiled in water to make a beverage. Seeds were ground into a paste similar to peanut butter that was rolled into balls and carried while traveling. Seed hulls were made into black, gray, blue, and purple dyes to color baskets, pottery, and fabrics. Golden sunflower petals and pollen were used to paint faces for ceremonial dances. Oil from the seeds was used in cooking and to condition hair and skin.

By the time Columbus landed in the New World, sunflowers with big heads and seeds were being grown by tribes across the continent from the Northeast to the Southwest. The SENECA, for example, is a variety still in existence today that can trace its historical roots to the Seneca tribe of New York. Spanish explorers carried sunflower seeds from New Mexico to Spain in the beginning of the 16th century. First grown in the Old World as ornamentals, sunflowers spread from Madrid to the botanic gardens of other European capitals. When they reached Russia in the 18th century, it was the beginning of a beautiful friendship.

Sunflowers rapidly became an important food crop in Russia because their oil could be eaten during Lent and other periods of religious fasting. They had arrived at the doors of the Russian Orthodox Church too late to be classified as a forbidden food. During the 18th and 19th centuries, Russian agriculturists improved sunflowers as a food crop by selecting seeds for their valuable traits. By the middle of the 1800s, sunflower fields covered vast areas from Ukraine to Siberia, and everybody walked around with a pocketful of sunflower seeds for snacking.

At the end of the 19th century, these improved sunflowers were brought back to North America by Russian immigrants. At first they were mainly grown for silage for animals, but early in this century, they began to be grown for oil. By the 1970s, consumers discovered the taste and healthy aspects of sunflower seeds; varieties were improved still more, and production rapidly increased. By the 1990s, there were 2.6 million acres of sunflowers planted in the United States annually, yielding about 1,138 pounds of seeds per acre.

Today sunflower production is centered in the northern Great Plains. North Dakota raises about 1.4 million acres annually, or more than half of the national total. South Dakota plants about 500,000 acres; Minnesota about 300,000; Kansas about 150,000; and Colorado about 75,000. Most of the sunflower seeds are processed for oil, which is mainly used as a cooking oil or to make margarine but also has industrial uses in paint, varnish, plastics, and diesel fuel. About 35 percent of the sunflower seed crop is used to feed humans, livestock, or birds.

The sunflower is the fifth-largest oilseed crop in the world.

SUNFLOWERS CITED

"The first seed that we planted in the spring was a sunflower seed. Ice breaks on the Missouri about the first week of April; and we planted sunflower seed as soon after as the soil could be worked. Our native name for the lunar month that corresponds most nearly to April is Mapi'-o'cē-mi'di, or Sunflower-planting-moon.... We thought a field surrounded by a...row of sunflowers, had a handsome appearance."

—*From* Buffalo Bird Woman's Garden, Agriculture of the Hidatsa Indians, *as told to Gilbert L. Wilson, Minnesota Historical Society Press; St. Paul, 1987.*

"*Helianthus annuas* [*sic*].—Garden Sun-flower [*sic*]. This lordly plant is too well known to need any description."

    —*From* Flower-Garden; or, Breck's Book of Flowers *by Joseph Breck, originally published by John P. Jewett & Co., Boston, 1851; republished by OPUS Publications, Inc., Guilford, Connecticut, 1988.*

· The prairie sunflower *(Helianthus petiolaris* Nutt.) "looks rather like a field daisy trying to be a sunflower and not succeeding too well."

    —*Edgar Anderson in* Plants, Man, and Life, *University of California Press, Berkeley, 1952.*

SOURCES

FOR ANNUAL SUNFLOWERS

W. Atlee Burpee Co.
300 Park Ave.
Warminster, PA 18974
(800) 888-1447

The Cook's Garden
P.O. Box 53528
Londonderry, VT 05148
(802) 824-3400

William Dam Seeds
P.O. Box 8400
Dundas, ON
Canada L9H 6M1

Johnny's Selected Seeds
Foss Hill Road
Albion, ME 04910
(207) 437-4301

Native Seeds/SEARCH
2509 N. Campbell Ave.
Tucson, AZ 85719
(602) 327-9123

Park Seed Co.
Cokesbury Road
Greenwood, SC 29647
(800) 845-3369

Seeds of Change
P.O. Box 15700
Santa Fe, NM 87506
(505) 438-8080

Southern Exposure
Seed Exchange
P.O. Box 170
Earlysville, VA 22936
(804) 973-4703

FOR ANNUAL SUNFLOWERS, continued

Territorial Seed Co.
Box157
Cottage Grove, OR 97424
(503) 942-9547

FOR PERENNIAL SUNFLOWERS

Andre Viette Farm
Route 1, Box 16
Fishersville, VA 22939
(703) 943-2315

Niche Gardens
1111 Dawson Road
Chapel Hill, NC 27516
(919) 967-0078

Prairie Moon Nursery
Route 2, Box 163
Winona, MN 55987
(507) 462-1362

Prairie Nursery
P.O. Box 306
Westfield WI 53964
(608) 296-3679

Prairie Ridge Nursery
9738 Overland Road
Mt. Horeb, WI 53572
(608) 437-5245

Shooting Star Nurseries
444 Bates Road
Frankfort, KY 40601
(502) 223-1679